THE MOST Disgusting Foods ON THE PLANET

BY JOHN PERRITANO

CAPSTONE PRESS
a capstone imprint

Velocity is published by Capstone Press,
151 Good Counsel Drive, P.O. Box 669, Mankato, Minnesota 56002.
www.capstonepub.com

Books published by Capstone Press are manufactured with paper
containing at least 10 percent post-consumer waste.

Library of Congress Cataloging-in-Publication Data
Perritano, John.
  The most disgusting foods on the planet / By John Perritano.
    p. cm.—(Velocity. disgusting stuff)
  Includes bibliographical references and index.
  Summary: "Discusses gross foods from around the world"—Provided by publisher.
  ISBN 978-1-4296-7534-5 (library binding) 1. Curiosities and wonders—Juvenile literature.
  2. Food—Miscellanea—Juvenile literature. 3. Aversion—Miscellanea—Juvenile literature.
  I. Title.
  AG243.P368 2012
  394.1'2—dc23

                                                        2011029257

Editor: Barbara Linde
Project Manager: Archna Bisht
Art Director: Suzan Kadribasic
Designer: Ankita Sharma, Manish Kumar
Image Researcher: Ranjana Batra

Photo Credits
Alamy: Peter Treanor, cover, Blammo, title, Victor Korchenko, 8-9, Classic Image, 18, Ken Tam,
20-21, Catherine Brown, 24-25, Olga A. Kolos, 34 (bottom), David Curtis, 34-35, Urban Golob,
39 (bottom); AP Images: Katsumi Kasahara, 28-29; Fotolia: The physicist, 6-7, Paris Photo, 12-13;
Getty Images: China Photos/Getty Images News, 6; iStockphoto: Orange PhotoGraphic, 13 (top),
Danielthomson, 19 (top), David Ciemny 32-33, Antagain, 36-37; Photolibrary: 42-43, Peter Menzel/
Science Photo Library, 4, Frans Lemmens/Lineair, 11 (top), Matthias Baumgartner, 38-39; Science
Photo Library: Merlin Tuttle, 22-23, Fred Mcconnaughey, 28 (bottom); Shutterstock: 2-3, 18-19,
Sven Schermer, 6, 28-29, 44-45 (top), 48, Chad Zuber, 10-11, Filipe B. Varela, 12-13 (top), Jiri
Hera, 14-15, Shi Yali, 16-17, Lagui 26-27, Jean Schweitzer, 27, Doug Matthews, 30-31, Baloncici,
34-35, Eric Isselee, 36-37 (top), Carlos Arranz, 38 (bottom), szefei, 44-45; Spectrum Photofile: 40;
Thinkstock: iStockphoto, 5

Printed in the United States of America in Stevens Point, Wisconsin.
102011   006404WZS12

Table of Contents

Something's Moving on My Plate!

What's for lunch? Pizza or a steaming bowl of saliva soup? You might say pizza. Others might order the soup.

Some people eat fish heads. Others find grasshoppers tasty. A food that you think is gross may be delicious to someone else.

In different parts of the world, different foods are acceptable and popular. Some eat certain types of foods because it is part of their culture or religion. What you think is weird is normal for others. In Vermont, cheddar cheese rules! In China, many people think cheese is disgusting. Who doesn't like a juicy hamburger? Hindus don't. To them, cows are sacred.

We eat food to give us energy and to be healthy. We eat because it makes us feel good. Mealtime is a chance to be with our friends and family. But some foods are not as appetizing as others.

Pull up a plate and try not to lose your appetite. It's time to discover the most disgusting foods on the planet!

saliva—the clear liquid in the mouth of a person or animal that helps with swallowing and digestion

culture—a people's way of life, ideas, art, customs, and traditions

Chapter 1

Bugs à la Carte

Bugs are creepy. Bugs are crawly. But for some, bugs aren't just for swatting. They make a nice snack!

bee larva

Bzzzz

Bees buzz and bees sting. They make gooey honey. But did you know that some people think bees are tasty?

Thailand is a nation in Southeast Asia. People in many countries love to eat Thai food. One thing you probably won't see on a menu at a Thai restaurant in the United States is bee larvae. But it is a popular food in Thailand and other Asian countries.

Bee larvae look like the tiny worms you might feed a pet lizard. Bee larvae are high in protein. People need protein to build strong bones and muscles.

Some bee larvae are packaged with the bee hive. One way to eat the insects is to break a chunk off the hive and eat it like a cookie. *Crunch!* Cooks also wrap the larvae in banana leaves and grill them. Some people put soy sauce on the tiny bees before eating them.

larva—an insect at the stage of development between an egg and a pupa when it looks like a worm; more than one larva are larvae

Crispy Caterpillars

Would you eat a caterpillar? Probably not, but in Africa, the critters are popular munchies.

Don't say "yuck" just yet. Caterpillars are very healthy. They are packed with protein and low in fat. They're also rich in vitamins and minerals like iron. Iron helps the body use oxygen.

Caterpillars are an important source of food in Africa. People grind dried caterpillars into flour. Cooks add the critters to stews and fry them as snacks.

Caterpillars are an important **industry** in parts of Africa too. In Malawi and other African nations, people harvest caterpillars. Caterpillars live on trees. Up to 7 pounds (3 kilograms) of caterpillars can be collected from a single tree! The harvested caterpillars are sold in the local markets.

industry—a single branch of business or trade

Beastly Biscuits

Beginning in the 1400s, sailors often spent months at sea. They had very little to eat. Often, the only food they had was what they brought with them. Sailors brought salted pork and other meat. If they were lucky, they might find some fruit on a tropical island.

However, most meals consisted of nothing but cracker-like biscuits called "hard tack." Sailors waited until dark to eat the hard tack. Why? They didn't want to see the worms crawling in the food.

Bugs with an Odor

They melt in your mouth and stink in your hand.

Stink bugs spice up food. To many people, they're also great as a snack. Why does a stink bug stink? The bugs give off an awful odor when they sense danger.

The six-legged creatures are considered a tasty dish in Mexico. One day a year, the residents of Taxco, Mexico, race into the woods in search of stink bugs. They pluck the bugs from under rocks and logs and stuff them into bags. The race is part of the Dia del Jumil. The race takes place on the first Monday after the Day of the Dead Festival, which is held on November 1st and 2nd.

After the race, the live bugs are thrown in pots of warm water. When the pots are stirred, everyone holds their noses. The bugs release a revolting odor. The smell hurts everyone's eyes. Finally, the bugs are boiled and dried in the sun.

But Mexicans don't eat stink bugs just on Dia del Jumil. They eat them all the time. Sometimes they even put the bugs in tacos and salsa.

Stink bugs are also eaten in other parts of the world. In Africa, people pop the heads off the bugs, squeeze their stomachs, and watch the green slime ooze out. Then they wipe the gunk on a rock and pop the critters in their mouths!

FACT

A serving of stink bugs has more protein than an equal-sized serving of beef.

Chapter 2

Sickening Sides

How about some tasty chicken butt as an appetizer? Or maybe goat dung oil for dipping? The world is full of sickening side dishes.

Goat Dung Oil

Oil is made out of olives. Oil is made out of peanuts and sesame seeds. In Morocco, people make oil from goat poop!

Morocco is a country in North Africa. The argan tree is one of a few plants that grow in the Moroccan desert. The tree produces plum-sized nuts that are rich in oil. Climbing the tree is one way to pick argan nuts. Another way is to let goats do the work. Yes, goats climb trees!

In the summer when the nuts are ripe, the goats climb up and eat the nuts. People wait for the goats to poop. Then they pick through the poop to find the nuts that the goats have digested. The nuts are then washed and pressed until the oil seeps out.

Some people who make argan oil to sell don't wait for the goats to digest the nuts first. They pick the nuts themselves. Argan nut oil is used to fry food. It is also used to flavor other foods. Moroccans sprinkle the oil on top of tomato salads. They also use it in stews. Argan oil sold to the public costs the buyers up to $120 a quart!

argan nuts

Cutting the Cheese

What's your favorite cheese? Cheddar? Swiss? American? How about head cheese?

Head cheese is very popular in many countries. But head cheese isn't really cheese at all. It's jellied meat from the head of a pig, sheep, or cow.

Once the animal has been slaughtered, the cooks remove the head, shave it, and throw it into a pot of boiling water. People often put the animal's tongue and hooves into the pot as well. They then add onion, pepper, salt, and vinegar.

When the meat is done cooking, it is picked off the bones and poured into a large pan. As it cools, the head cheese becomes a solid. Head cheese looks like a big sausage.

FACT

Cooks in Louisiana season their head cheese, known as souse, with vinegar and hot sauce.

Chewing the Fat

Raw Bar

If you like foods that squirm, order raw octopus. Like its cousin the squid, an octopus has no bones. Its eight arms are fleshy and chewy. The meat is so tough that some cooks beat it with a mallet to soften it. Baby octopus is a more tender treat. People cut it into small, bite-sized chunks and gobble it up.

Chicken is a popular food all over the world.

For many chicken-lovers, fried drumsticks are a lip-smacking treat. Many people love to eat chicken wings smothered in hot sauce. Chicken breast is used in many recipes. But one part of the bird doesn't get much respect—the chicken butt.

Known as "Bishop's Nose," the rear end of a chicken is a common dish in Asia. Bishop's Nose is mostly fat, but many people think that it is very tasty. The meat is tender and easy to chew. Cooks fry or grill the heart-shaped butt and serve it on a stick.

FACT

The name "Bishop's Nose" also refers to the butt of other fowl, such as turkeys and ducks.

Chapter 3
Stomach-~~///~~ Turning Soups

Some grandmas make chicken or vegetable soup. Other grandmas use whatever is available, including the lungs of a goat or a pigeon.

Gruesome Goat Soup

What did you eat for breakfast this morning?
Cereal? Bacon and eggs? An English muffin?

In Tanzania, a special soup called *supu* is the main course at breakfast time. Sound delicious? It is—if you like soup made from goat lungs, hearts, and livers.

Some cooks add chili peppers, onions, and garlic to the broth, which is made with water. Some people make goat soup with tomatoes or plantains, which are like bananas. Cooks sometimes add flavor with coconut milk or curry powder.

The Maasai live in Tanzania and other parts of East Africa. When a Maasai woman has had a baby, her husband might make a pot of goat soup for breakfast. The soup is rich in vitamins and minerals that help keep her healthy. Goat soup is also made in Liberia, Nigeria, and other African nations.

What's Not to Lichen?

People eat anything when they are starving. That was true for George Washington and his troops as they fought the British during the American Revolution (1775-1783). The winter of 1777-1778 was cold and brutal. At the time, Washington and his men were camping at Valley Forge, Pennsylvania.

There was so little to eat that the troops scraped lichen from rocks. Lichen is made up of fungi and tiny water plants. Washington's men boiled the lichen and made a soup called rock tripe. The soup was high in calories, and it helped the troops get through the cold winter.

fungi—organisms that have no leaves, flowers, or roots; mushrooms and molds are fungi
calorie—a measurement of the amount of energy that food gives you

Beastly Broth

In China there's nothing yummier than a bowl of saliva soup.

The soup is made from the nests of swiftlets, which are common birds in Asia. The tiny birds live in dark caves. Like other birds, swiftlets use twigs to build their nests. But they also include saliva!

It's not easy to grab hold of swiftlet nests. They are usually stuck to the walls of caves. The nests are cleaned in water and then dried and sold in markets. Restaurant cooks often simmer the nests in chicken broth. The cooked nests look like clear noodles. The soup has a jellylike texture. Some call the dish saliva soup. Others call it bird's nest soup.

FACT

Humans harvest about 20 million swiftlet nests each year. However, the birds are not harmed. The nests are collected after they have been used by the birds.

The bird's nest is cooked with water and rock sugar to make a bird's nest dessert soup.

Fruit Bat
Soup

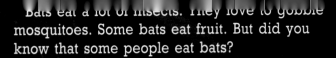

Bats eat a lot of insects. They love to gobble mosquitoes. Some bats eat fruit. But did you know that some people eat bats?

Fruit bat soup is a **delicacy** in Micronesia, a country made up of islands in the western Pacific Ocean. Preparing fruit bat soup is a lot like cooking a lobster. Cooks put live fruit bats into a pot of boiling water. They add onions, ginger, and salt. Some cooks pick the meat off the cooked bats. They put the meat back into the broth and discard the skin. Other cooks serve the whole bat in the soup dish. Coconut milk or soy sauce are often added to both versions of the soup.

High-Flying Soup

Take the meat from a pigeon and 0.5 pounds (227 grams) of veal. Add 2 quarts (1.9 liters) of water. Add some seasoning, such as salt and pepper. Bring to a boil. Simmer for an hour. In no time you will have pigeon soup. Pigeon soup is on many menus throughout the world. Russian cooks make pigeon soup by adding the bird meat to beef broth. In Great Britain cooks serve the soup with crusty rolls.

delicacy—a rare or prized item of food

Chapter 4
Detestable Drinks

What do you wash your food down with? Milk? Juice? Water? How about cow pee or eel soda? In some countries both are on the menu.

Poo Coffee

One coffee company says that its brew is good to the last drop. Some coffee is good to the last poop!

The poopy coffee comes from Indonesia. Its name is *Kopi Luwak*. You probably won't find Kopi Luwak at your local donut shop. The coffee sells for as much as $600 a pound!

People harvest Kopi Luwak with help from a catlike animal called the palm civet. People used to think the animals were pests. They climbed coffee trees and ate the ripest coffee beans. Over time, people figured out how to make cash from the palm civets' pesky habits.

After they eat the coffee beans, palm civets poop near rocks and tree stumps. The beans, still whole, come out in the poop. People pick the beans out of the poop. They wash and dry the beans. Then they brew the beans into a delicious coffee.

What gives Kopi Luwak such a great taste? Enzymes in the animal's digestive system mix with the beans and give the coffee its flavor.

enzyme—a protein that helps break down food
digestive system—the group of organs responsible for breaking down food into energy for the body and for getting rid of waste

Cow Cola

Which cola tastes better? Some people say Coke. Others say Pepsi.

In India there is a cola made of cow **urine** called *gau jal*, which means "cow water." The drink is not popular throughout India. People who do drink it do so for religious reasons or because they believe that it is healthy.

Gau jal does not taste like pee. And it doesn't smell like pee. It is also not carbonated like other colas. But it does contain natural herbs, and its creators say it tastes good.

Horsing Around

Cow's milk is a staple of many people's diets. But did you know that some people milk horses? Milk from a mare is called *kumis*, and it is popular in Mongolia and other Central Asian countries.

The kumis is left out for a few days before it is ready to drink. This practice allows **bacteria** to grow. The bacteria create acid. The acid makes the kumis slightly bubbly. Kumis is usually served cold.

urine—liquid waste that people and animals pass through their bodies

bacteria—one-celled, microscopic living things that exist all around you and inside you; many bacteria are useful, but some cause disease

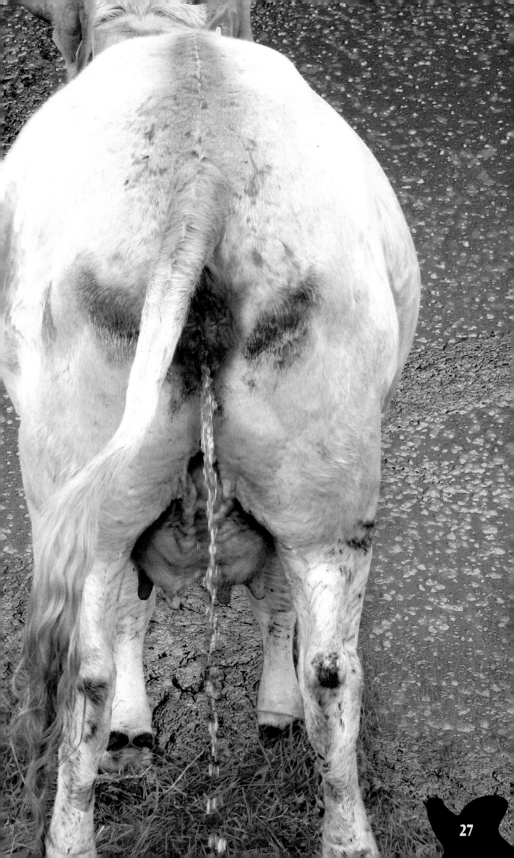

Fizzy Eel

Lemonade is refreshing on a hot summer day. So is a can of eel soda.

Believe it or not, eel soda is a drink in Japan. The soda is called *Unagi Nobori*. That means "surging eel" in English. Some say drinking eel soda in the summer cools them down and gives them energy.

The fizzy soda uses flavoring taken from eels. The extract is made from the head, liver, spleen, and other parts of the eel. But don't think eel soda will taste like your favorite ginger ale or root beer. Eel soda tastes like … well, broiled eel!

FACT

Some people say the texture of eel is like eating rubber bands and that the flavor is like mushrooms.

Salad Soda

Eel soda is not the only unusual soda sold in Japan. For several years, Coca-Cola has been selling a soft drink called Water Salad. It's made from vegetables and water. In the summer of 2007, Pepsi produced a special drink called Pepsi Ice Cucumber. Yes, it tasted like cucumbers!

Chapter 5

Rotten Entrees

Moose nose for supper? Monkey brains for lunch? In many countries, these main dishes are considered extremely tasty!

The Nose Knows

Native Alaskans used animal skins for clothes. They used animal bones as tools. No part of the animal went to waste, not even the nose!

A popular dish in parts of Alaska is still jellied moose nose. But jellied moose nose has nothing in common with the jelly you put on your peanut butter sandwich!

Recipe for
Snotty Snouts

1. The first thing to do is remove the dead moose's upper jaw. Then throw the moose snout in a pot of boiling water. The water makes it easier to pull the moose's hair out.

2. Once you clean the hair off of the snout, put it in a pot of fresh water. Add some onions, garlic, and spices. Cook until the meat is tender. Take the snout out of the pan. Save the broth and the meat. Throw away the bones. Slice the snout and layer it in a loaf pan. Let everything cool overnight.

3. Now comes the jelly part. Reheat the broth. Pour it over the cold moose snout. The "jelly" will cool and firm up. It looks like petroleum jelly. Serve the jellied moose snout cold.

Brain
Food

Mongolian Boodog

People living in Mongolia include many kinds of meat in their cuisine. One of their favorite meals is boodog. Boodog is a dish made from goats or marmots. A marmot is a big squirrel. Mongolian chefs cook the meat by putting hot stones in the dead animal's stomach. The stones cook the animal from the inside out.

In the movie *Indiana Jones and the Temple of Doom*, chilled monkey brains are served as a dessert in a scene set in India. But no one eats monkey brains in real life ... or do they?

Yes, they do! It's an ancient custom in several countries, including China and Cambodia. People hunt monkeys for all kinds of reasons, but some believe eating the animal's brain is healthy and can even cure some medical problems. Eating monkey brains can actually make people ill. That's because some monkeys might be sick. Diseases can be passed on to the person who eats the brains.

In many areas monkeys could soon become endangered. Some groups are trying to stop people from hunting monkeys for food.

cuisine—style of cooking
endangered—at risk of dying out

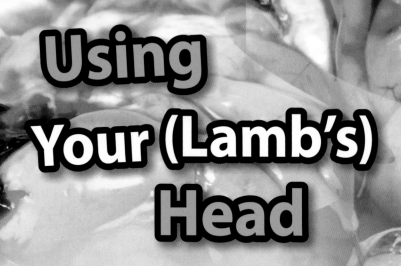

Using Your (Lamb's) Head

In some countries, lamb chops are served with mint jelly. In Iceland lamb is prepared a different way.

A popular dish in Iceland is lamb's head, or *svio*. Cooking svio is not an easy job. First, the lamb's head is salted. Then it sits for a week. Afterward, the wool is removed. The head is then boiled in salt water. The dish is finished when the flesh slides off the bone. Svio is often served with boiled potatoes and rutabagas.

The meat can also be made into jam. The jam is known as *brawn*. Brawn can be used as a topping for bread or in a sandwich.

Sheep heads are also used to make svio.

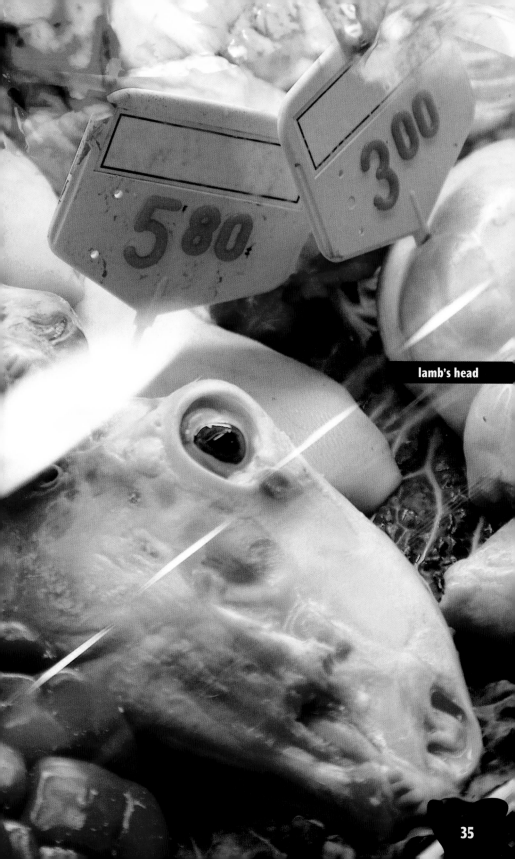

lamb's head

Appetizing Amphibians

FACT

The French eat 3,000 to 4,000 tons (2,700 to 3,600 metric tons) of frog legs each year. Most of these legs come from frogs raised in other countries like Indonesia.

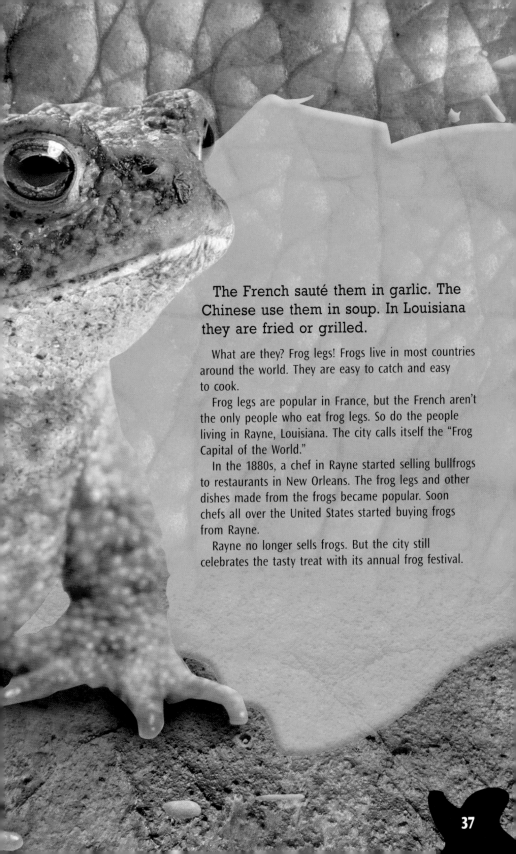

The French sauté them in garlic. The Chinese use them in soup. In Louisiana they are fried or grilled.

What are they? Frog legs! Frogs live in most countries around the world. They are easy to catch and easy to cook.

Frog legs are popular in France, but the French aren't the only people who eat frog legs. So do the people living in Rayne, Louisiana. The city calls itself the "Frog Capital of the World."

In the 1880s, a chef in Rayne started selling bullfrogs to restaurants in New Orleans. The frog legs and other dishes made from the frogs became popular. Soon chefs all over the United States started buying frogs from Rayne.

Rayne no longer sells frogs. But the city still celebrates the tasty treat with its annual frog festival.

Smelly Fish Treats

If you are hungry for a treat, try this recipe: Grab hold of five or six salmon heads. Bury them in the backyard and let them sit for days. Dig them up and eat them raw.

It's no surprise that Alaskans call this dish "stink heads." In some parts of Alaska, salmon are used to make fish heads. In other towns, whitefish is used. They are equally smelly.

The fish heads are a traditional meal for native Alaskans. The food is even on the menu of some restaurants.

The fish is usually buried in wooden barrels or plastic bags. The heads sit for days and rot. What makes animal flesh rot? Bacteria. That's why there is a problem with the stinky treat. People can get food poisoning from eating the fish heads.

Chapter 6

Disgusting Desserts

There is nothing like a sweet treat to finish off a meal. But if you think dessert is the best part of a meal, think again.

Let It Snow

Snow jelly for dessert. Doesn't sound disgusting at all.

But don't let the innocent name fool you. Snow jelly is made from the internal organs of an Asiatic grass frog in northern China. The Koreans call the dessert *hashima* or *hasma*.

Cooks mix the frog organs with sugar and then steam the mixture until it is cooked. After spending seven to 10 days in the refrigerator, hashima is ready to eat.

Some people put a spoonful in milk or tea. Others put it on top of spinach. It is also used to make soups sweet. Some say hashima tastes like tapioca pudding.

Hashima is healthy and high in protein. Some people believe that eating snow jelly is good for the lungs and liver. Some even think it can make skin look better.

FACT

Snow jelly looks like jelly made from fruit. Both have the same texture.

Chocolate- Covered Critters

Many people love chocolate. Chocolate candy? Yum! Chocolate ice cream? Delicious! Chocolate milk? Tasty! Chocolate insects? Hmmm ...

Eating insects is common throughout the world. Africans eat hundreds of different kinds of insects. Bugs are popular in South and Central America too. Vendors often sell the insects on street corners in these parts of the world.

But if you have never tried eating an insect before, you might want to start with one that is chocolate-covered. How about a package of chocolate-covered grasshoppers? Or would you like to try chocolate-covered crickets? If you just want a small snack, try chocolate-covered ants!

And if you aren't a chocolate lover, you can still enjoy buggy desserts. Many candy stores in Mexico and other parts of Central America sell bug lollipops. The lollipops are sweet just like any lollipop, except they have crickets, ants, and other bugs inside. How many licks does it take to get to the cricket in the center of a lollipop? Who knows? But have fun finding out!

Wiggly Snack

Worms aren't just for fishing anymore. Larvets
Worm Snax are edible farm-raised worms that
have been dried to make them crispy. They have
fewer calories than potato chips—and just as much
crunch! The snacks come in a variety of flavors,
including barbecue and cheddar cheese.

The Smelly Fruit

If you like fruit, you might love durian. Just hold your nose!

Some people say durian stinks like old socks. Others say it smells like baby poop. Others say it reeks of rotten, mushy onions.

Whatever it smells like, the fruit's odor is so bad that in some places eating durian in public is banned. There are signs on buses in Singapore that say, "No loud music. No smoking. No durian!" But durian is actually quite popular in Southeast Asia. While tourists might run away after smelling the fruit, many local people enjoy it.

Durian is spiky and big, about 12 inches (30 centimeters) long. The fruit grows in trees and is sold in markets throughout Southeast Asia. To eat a durian, you cut it in half and scoop out the flesh. It can be made into chips and jam.

Appetizing or Disgusting?

Hopefully you didn't lose your appetite during this disgusting dining jaunt. Which food was the most revolting to you? Which one was the least sickening? Remember that no matter how gross something sounds to you, someone else probably likes it. Maybe someday you'll try a food that disgusts you now!

GLOSSARY

bacteria (bak-TEER-ee-uh)—one-celled, microscopic living things that exist all around you and inside you; many bacteria are useful, but some cause disease

calorie (KAL-ur-ee)—a measurement of the amount of energy that food gives you

cuisine (kwi-ZEEN)—style of cooking

culture (KUHL-chur)—a people's way of life, ideas, art, customs, and traditions

delicacy (DEL-i-kuh-see)—a rare or prized item of food

digestive system (dye-JES-tiv SIS-tuhm)—the group of organs responsible for breaking down food into energy for the body and for getting rid of waste

endangered (in-DAYN-juhrd)—at risk of dying out

enzyme (EN-zime)—a protein that helps break down food

fungi (FUHN-jy)—organisms that have no leaves, flowers, or roots; mushrooms and molds are fungi

industry (IN-duh-stree)—a single branch of business or trade

larva (LAR-vuh)—insect at the stage of development between an egg and a pupa when it looks like a worm; more than one larva are larvae

saliva (suh-LYE-vuh)—the clear liquid in the mouth of a person or animal that helps with swallowing and digestion

urine (YOOR-uhn)—liquid waste that people and animals pass through their bodies

READ MORE

Johanson, Paula. *Fake Foods: Fried, Fast, and Processed: The Disgusting Story.* Incredibly Disgusting Food. New York: Rosen Central, 2011.

Leet, Karen. *Food Intruders: Invisible Creatures Lurking in Your Food.* Tiny Creepy Creatures. Mankato, Minn.: Capstone Press, 2012.

Miller, Connie Colwell. *This Book Might Make You Gag: A Collection of Crazy Gross Trivia.* Ultimate Trivia Collection. Mankato, Minn.: Capstone Press, 2012.

INTERNET SITES

FactHound offers a safe, fun way to find Internet sites related to this book. All of the sites on FactHound have been researched by our staff.

Here's all you do:

Visit *www.facthound.com*

Type in this code: 9781429675345

INDEX